1 MONTH OF
FREE
READING

at
www.ForgottenBooks.com

By purchasing this book you are
eligible for one month membership to
ForgottenBooks.com, giving you
unlimited access to our entire
collection of over 1,000,000 titles via
our web site and mobile apps.

To claim your free month visit:
www.forgottenbooks.com/free503785

ISBN 978-0-483-98746-3
PIBN 10503785

This book is a reproduction of an important historical work. Forgotten Books uses state-of-the-art technology to digitally reconstruct the work, preserving the original format whilst repairing imperfections present in the aged copy. In rare cases, an imperfection in the original, such as a blemish or missing page, may be replicated in our edition. We do, however, repair the vast majority of imperfections successfully; any imperfections that remain are intentionally left to preserve the state of such historical works.

DOUBTS AND DIFFICULTIES OF NATIONAL UNITY.

RESS

FORE

THE ALUMNI SOCIETY

OF THE

niversit o G orgia,

JUNE 18th, 1895.

By MARION J. VERDERY,

OF NEW YORK.

AUGUSTA, GA.
Chronicle Job Printing Company.
1895.

CORRESPONDENCE.

Hon. M. J. Verdery,

MY DEAR SIR:—It gives me pleasure to carry out my instructions as Secretary of the Alumni Society of the University of Georgia in transmitting to you the following resolution of thanks, passed unani- mously by the Society in recognition of your kindness to them on June 18th last:

Resolved, That the thanks of this Society are due, and are hereby warmly tendered to Hon. Marion J. Verdery, of New York, for the admirable address to which we have just listened, and that the Secre- tary of the Society be instructed to request a copy of the same for pub- lication.

This resolution was passed at the meeting of the Alumni Society immediately succeeding the address, and in behalf of the Society I trust that you will kindly furnish me with a copy for publication.

Very respectfully,

DAVID C. BARROW, JR.

Secretary.

ATHENS, GA., June 20th, 1895.

Prof. David C. Barrow, Jr., Secretary Alumni Society, University of Georgia, Athens, Ga.

MY DEAR SIR:—Your courteous note of this date, communicating to me the flattering resolution adopted by the Alumni Society, and requesting, in accordance with the resolution, a copy of my address, delivered before the Society on the 18th instant, is received.

In compliance with the request, I send you the manuscript here- with and with grateful acknowledgments to the Society and to you, I remain

Yours respetfully,

M. J. VERDERY.

ADDRESS.

Mr. President and Members of the Alumni Society:

LADIES AND GENTLEMEN:—I know this to be a proper form of salutation, but it is not altogether to my liking. I should very much prefer to adopt the good old-fashioned Methodist formula, and say, dearly beloved brethren and sisters. As a matter of fact I really do feel almost akin to everybody in this audience, but however I might address you, my lips would be false to my heart if with my first breath I did not say, thank you. I am not only grateful for the honor you have done me in inviting me to deliver this address, but I am grateful because your invitation has called me once again back to Georgia. I tell you, my friends, until a thousand miles have stretched between you and the scenes of your childhood, your soul can never give full tone to the echo of that dear old song,

> Take me back to the place where I first saw the light,
>   To the sweet sunny South take me home,
> Where the mocking bird sang me to rest every night,
>   Ah! why was I tempted to roam?"

I am determined not to be hampered on this occasion by any lurking consciousness of relative unworthiness, but, on the contrary, have concluded to appropriate Judge Bleckley's theory, who under similar circumstances, remarked that "whenever he had an honor done him, the less worthy of it he felt, the keener was his enjoyment in accepting it." The paramount thought with me at this moment is the precious one that I am here,—here in Georgia,—here in Athens,—here on the blessed old Campus,—here in the embrace of friendly love that has outlasted the years, and with a fervent God-bless you welling up in my heart, I say again, thank you.

It has been more than a quarter of a century since I stood on this platform, and yet the scenes of that day are as fresh to me as if they had been enacted yesterday. My fancy is a wing, flying back through the shadowy yesterdays of many years; my mind is a medley of memories chiming in sweetest harmony with the music of long ago; my eyes are shut, and yet I see faces that will never fade from the picture gallery of my heart; my ears are stopped, but oh how plainly I hear the happy voices of the boys and girls who were the boon companions of my College days. Blessed days, so long gone that the girls of then are the mothers of now, and the boys have come to wear the silver crowns of middle age. And yet, how near it all seems. Why, the echo of that whirlwind of applause which followed Albert Cox's memorable speech delivered from this stage nearly thirty years ago rings in my ears at this moment, and the exquisite imagery of blessed Grady's "Castles in Air" is as beautiful to mind today as it was when I heard him speak the prose poem.

Oh, memory, priceless gift of God, storehouse for treasures that can be kept nowhere else; yea, storehouse like Heaven itself, where neither moth nor rust doth corrupt, and where thieves do not break through and steal;" thy doors are without locks, and yet, whispers of tenderness, snatches of song, dreams of love, pictures of beauty and even the perfume of flowers are stored there in safety forever. You know when Ann of Austria confessed her love to the Duke of Buckingham, his Grace dropped a jewel by the wayside, saying, that he wanted some foot-traveler to find the gem, and thereby be made glad at the place where he had found his greatest joy.

I never had occasion to drop any jewel anywhere in Athens for precisely the same reason that the Duke of

Buckingham flung his down in the public road, but if I had dropped a gem at every spot where I told some Ann of Athens what I thought of her, Cobbham would have been paved like a street of the New Jerusalem, and it would pay today to rake any front yard in Athens and sift the dirt for precious stones.

But I am talking a long way off from my subject, and this is not an occasion to be wholly given over to reminiscences. When I was striving to determine what my subject should be, I wrote to my very dear friend, W. W. Thomas, and asked him what I should talk about; he replied promptly, saying that he didn't care at all what I talked about, but that there were just two things which I must not do,—first, I must not speak too long, and secondly, I must not make a "speech under the third head." This was his explanation of a "speech under the third head." He said several years ago a gentleman delivered an address here, and the day after, when Governor Brown and Dr. H. V. M. Miller and Hon. Nat. Hammond were going back to Atlanta together, Dr. Miller asked Governor Brown what he thought of the address the day before. The Governor replied that he thought it was a speech under the third head; then they both laughed, but Colonel Hammond was not in the joke, and asked to be enlightened. Dr. Miller said that he and Governor Brown were once up near Tallulah Falls and went to hear an old hardshell Baptist minister, who took his text from St. Paul and proceeded with the sermon in this fashion: "Dearly beloved, I shall divide my sermon into three heads; under the first head I shall endeavor to show you what St. Paul did not mean. Under the second head I shall endeavor to show you what St. Paul did mean, and under the third head, I shall make a few general remarks on a line which I do not think St. Paul understood and which I know I do not.

I have determined to talk to you upon "The Doubts and Difficulties of National Unity,"

The subject naturally falls into an analysis something like this. Are there such doubts and are there such difficulties; and if so, are the former removable and the latter surmountable or not? No one can deny the existence of the doubts. They crop out in all parts of the country spasmodically in spiteful sayings and captious conduct, and confronted by numerous signs of distrust and discord, we cannot escape the question—is this county one country or not; if it is not, we should surely put a stop to all these after-dinner exuberances of feeling; we cannot be one country at a night feast, and widely separated in our feelings when the morning comes. But, on the other hand, if this is not one country and we are not one people, what mean the matchless messages of peace which have been borne North by Georgia's incomparable triumvirate, Grady, Gordon and Graves? If we are not one people in spirit and in sympathy, let Graves get no more into the very fastnesses of New England and pour out in matchless eloquence the story of complete reconciliation and Americanism, which the people of the South feel. If we are not one people, let us call home our superbest hero of the lost cause, John B. Gordon; call him home, I say, and bid him retract the generous tributes which I have repeatedly heard him pay to "the men who wore the blue," and bid him no more wrap himself in the stars and stripes in sign of his whole-souled loyalty, and claim at the same time that this dramatic act illustrates the hearts of his people. If we are not one people, let us stop our ears to the sweet echo of all the beautiful doctrines that were preached by the immortal Grady, who "died loving the nation into peace."

Secondly the difficulties of National Unity are undeniably great. The very fundamental idea of unity necessarily involves the thought of possible separation, and since throughout the universe it seems easier for things to drift apart than to pull together the difficulties of National Unity are multiform and complex.

In human nature the dominant principle is individualism or egoism—selfishness in other words. It is the most unconquerable passion in the world; there is nothing it will not do. It murders, it steals, it persecutes enemies, it betrays friends, it abuses charity and maligns virtue. It exiled Adam and Eve, it has been the pitfalls of kings, and the ruin of emperors. It cheats the devil and robs God. It spreads like pestilence, rendering families discordant, communities contentious and even the autonomy of nations uncertain. The splendor and magnificence of ancient Rome would be unmarred to day but for the selfish tyranny of Nero. The serpentine Seine, threading its way through the incomparable French capital, would never have run red with blood, and the awful horrors of the French Revolution would never have blotted the pages of human history, if National Unity had not been destroyed by political passion and selfish greed for personal gain. And our own blessed country would not, like the vail of the temple, have been rent in twain but for the bitterness of disagreement between the States, which, after all, in its last analysis, was a contention for the maintenance of selfish ends. And the temporary disruption of the States was so violent, and the calamitous cost thereof so inestimable, and the terrible consequences so lasting, that even at this late day—thirty years after the pipe of peace at Appomattox—it is still a question if the breach is thoroughly healed.

Now, it does seem to me, the sooner that question is settled by every man and woman of the land, the better. Let us settle it conscientiously and completely. It is a question for each separate individual. You cannot determine it for me, nor I for you. Is this an indissoluble nation or not? Is this vast expanse, from where the morning sun first kisses the hills of the East to where, when the day is gone, he goes down through the golden gate of the West, and from where the perpetual snows turban the mountain peaks of the far North down to the distant South where bridal wreaths of orange blossoms are in perpetual bloom; is this boundless estate only a sectionalized territory, or is it more than all else,—is it "America, the land of the free and the home of the brave?"

If we are not a unified people, bound together by all the possibilities of a common destiny and united by all the ties of kindred ambition, and sacredly joined in the name of true patriotism, then, for honor and truth's sake, let us quit all insincere speechmaking on special occasions.

I pray you will not misunderstand me. I do not charge the people of the South with any greater responsibility for the lack of National Unity than attaches to those of other parts of the country, but that there is lack of such unity is a fact beyond contradiction. It evidences itself up North. when some irresponsible scribbler or blatant blatherskite repudiates all professions of union and waves the bloody shirt. It crops out in fanatical and oftentimes hypocritical views in that section on the negro question. It shows itself in unmistakable jealousy of the South's power in national politics and vastness of her natural resources; but, then, the fault is not all there, the South in spirit and in speech is not altogether without sin against that consummation devoutly to be wished—a perfect National Unity.

We do not always seem to be dominated by that fundamental principle of patriotism, "the greatest good for the greatest number," and until we all, of every section, lift ourselves to that exalted plane of true citizenship, this union will only be a confederation of States—"distinct like the billows, but, alas! not one like the sea."

I know the difficulties in the way of an ideal union are great. The very vastness of our domain, variety of climate, diversity of occupation, the unlikeness of customs, and difference of education, all these conspire to create conflict of interest and drive asunder, rather than bind us together,

The solid South, aside from reverence for hallowed memories and sacred traditions, has stood unbroken so long, cnly because of the inherent strength that there is in unified local interests. But the days of the solid South are numbered. The South has been solid in opposition to the despicable and unpatriotic policy of that political faction which has prostituted itself in a thousand ways while masquerading in the name of the Republican party, and that faction was violently rebuked when the force bill was killed.

The future politics of this country are bound to revolve around great economic questions, and not to be warped by bitter memories and lingering prejudices. National achieve-ment is never accomplished along the line of passion and prejudice. Great living issues are upon, us, and as they press the South will divide, and the North, and the East, and the West will divide ; this will not be sectional division, but division within the sections ; every man's judgment leading him, in the light of his own intelligence, to conscientious convictions. Sooner or later what we have been calling the Democratic and Republican parties will be swallowed up in the birth of new parties. In this way the best intelligence all over the land will be enlisted under one banner, and the motto on that banner will be ''For the Sake of America.'' If this be not so, and the South is destined to be forever solid, what means the recent contest over the Governorship of Tennessee ? Why is North Carolina no longer a certain quantity in the solidity ? And how dare any man, and especially one with such ancestry as Thomas W. Sedden, the son of a member of Mr. Davis' last Cabinet, join an element in Alabama (the very cradle of Confederacy), which element swears to renounce Democracy rather than see the material interests of that State suffer. What a confirmation of Hancock's unhappy declaration, that the tariff was a local issue.

During the next Presidential campaign the questions

that will press hardest on every man for personal solution will not be whether he shall vote for a Republican or a Democrat, but whether he believes in protection or free trade, and what is the wisest and best solution of the currency question.

. You must realize, my dear people, that old issues are dead—not sentiments and traditions—far be it from me to suggest that the least of them should suffer the slightest forgetfulness. I would hold every tradition of this blessed Southland as precious as a sacred heritage, and I would rear our children in a knowledge of those happy days which made the old South what she was, and keep all those memories as sacred history of a civilization and social organism that has never had any parallel in the record of peoples. But as Ben Hill once said, "There was a South of secession and slavery; that South is gone. There is a South of energy, progress and power, which it behooves all her sons to guard jealously and build up triumphantly."

We must take hold of the issues that exist to-day. If the Southern people are to make themselves an influential factor in shaping the destiny of this great nation, they must prove themselves sound in political philosophy, wise in the science of economics and broad national policy. In the name of God let me beg you to steer clear of all isms! Stop your ears to the preaching of unwise leaders, who have political ambitions to serve and not patriotic purposes to promote. There are no men on the face of the earth, taken as a class, with clearer ideas of justice, fuller appreciation of wise legislation or better grounded in the principles of real statesmanship, than the men of the South, and yet you championed the "Income Tax." Why could you not see that one of its provisions alone was fatal to it. By what process of reasoning could you justify putting a $4,000 limit on incomes that were not to be taxed? Why was it not just as fair to make that limit $40,000. If you had insisted that all incomes (be they ever so infinitesimally small) should be taxed, you would have been beyond the reach even of the suspicion of assisting class legislation, and no man could have charged that you wanted a law which would reach a large class of people of other sections of the country, and yet let you escape. Now, the Income Tax has been repudiated by the highest tribunal of the land, and those who contended for it stand as the discredited advocates of an unconstitutional measure.

In a like manner, and I know in broaching this subject that I tread on dangerous ground,—in a like manner, I say, a great many of you are being badly advised and going wrong on money. Now, you will lose on that. Don't get mad because I tell you so; I am only speaking truth as I see it. It does seem to me that if there is any section of this whole country that could afford to be absolutely monometallists, and gold monometallists at that, the South is that section. Have you any silver mines ? Have you anything to sell that you cannot get gold for ? And has the amount of gold which you have heretofore gotten for what you sold ever been out of proportion to the quantity of other commodities which you could buy with that gold ? Is there any section of the country that raises any single product that will command as much gold even in the most depressed times, as the cotton crop of the South Do you not know that had it not been for this fact, the credit of the United States government could not have been maintained after the war. And yet there is all this talk about alliance with the West in order to secure free silver. Well, if you are going abroad to make any sectional alliance, in the name of Heaven lets make one in which there is some possibility of profit to you. You, the South ! with all your traditions, all your sacred memories, all your treasured stories, all your time-honored chivalry and heroism, all your blue-blooded aristocracy, with a past so rich that the history of it reads like romance, and memory of it makes the blood quicken with pride. You! with this character, and with this record, to talk about allying yourself to a people who have no past, no history, no tradition, only a mushroom present and an unassured future. You! who boast the most homogeneous people on the American continent, to join yourselves and your fortunes with a section that is the stronghold of anarchy and socialism ; you to ally yourselves to a people that have not much better sense of home and home-ties than the Arab in his tent, which he folds in the night and steals away. No! If there is to be any alliance, let us make a marriage worthy of our bride. All this silver twaddle is the veriest humbuggery. Do you know any process by which you are to immediately become enriched by the re-opening of the mints for unrestricted coinage of silver ? Has it never occurred to you that you cannot get any of those new silver dollars without giving a *quid pro quo* in exchange for them ; and then, who is advising you to adopt this propaganda as your financial deliverance ? Find me the strongest and best, the most intelligent and wisest six silver advocates that you know of in the South, and I will furnish you six names as worthy of trust as these and yet who vigorously dispute the wisdom of the silver policy.

I don't ask you to believe that free silver coinage is unwise because I say so, but let us test the question by the testimony of witnesses. I can name six men who would be enough to convert me, if I had never thought on the subject, or talked with any other man living but them ; I point you to six shining lights in the ranks of Democracy, with whom there has never been any variableness nor shadow of turning. I give you six men, all of whom have proven themselves competent in all respects to comprehend and judge any question of finance. They are not all Northerners nor all Southerners, but belong in equal numbers to the respective sections.

Do you know any better Democrat than Abram S. Hewitt, expert man of affairs, and profoundly learned statesman? He says: "Unrestricted coinage of silver would be ruinous."

Do you know any sounder Democrat than William C. Whitney, able in the counsels of the nation, wide in his experience on all economic questions, and learned in the mysteries of money? He says: "Free coinage of silver other than by fair international agreement, would be fatal to our national credit."

Has not J. Edward Simmons, for twenty years one of the leading Democrats of New York city, and President of the Fourth National Bank, one of the largest financial institutions of the metropolis—has he no claim upon your respectful attention? He says: "Unrestricted coinage of silver would put a chock under the wheels of this country's progress and result in such a shock to public credit that the consequences to all the material interests of the nation would be appalling." These are all Northerners.

Do you know any better Democrat, any more conspicuously successful man, any more prominent figure in the field of finance than R. T. Wilson? He says: "Unrestricted coinage of silver would blight all enterprise in the South, and be a relentless hindrance to the developments of its natural resources and general prosperity."

Do you know anybody who doubts the Democracy of John H. Inman? He says: "That the free silver craze has been instituted by a few political tricksters and a few Western miners, the former greedy for office and the latter greedy for gain."

Do you know why Samuel Spencer, born and reared in Columbus, Ga., and graduated from this very institution, a man standing today abreast with the foremost men of his profession, and managing the largest single property in the whole South; do you know why he should not be trusted as a man of truth, honesty and intelligence? He says: "This silver mania, if allowed to prevail, will prove the greatest engine for harm in the South that has ploughed that section since the war between the States devastated it."

Now, there you have three Northerners and three Southerners, all prominent, all successful, and each and every single one of them having more pecuniary interest in the South today than any two silverites in the whole section. Is this worth nothing? Ah! but some fellow who is joined to his idol cries back at me, yes, but they are all bondholders, they are rich, they are gold bugs. Well, suppose they are; does that argue them incompetent to discuss monetary propositions or currency systems?

Would you employ a man who had gone barefooted all his life to make your shoes, or engage a Zulu fresh from his native land to be your tailor? I believe silver agitation in the South comes in great measure from an opposition to the Administration, and that, in itself, ought to be enough to kill it. The man at the head of the Government today is the foremost living American and the only one the Democrats have ever been able to elect President since the war, and I fail to see where he has shown any lack of consideration, or given any evidence of prejudice against the Southern people. The presence of three Southerners in his Cabinet should be denial enough of any such insinuation.

But I do not mean by pointing out these discouraging signs of the times to admit that I am hopeless; I believe the perfect day will come. My faith is not based on any light which I claim to see gliding the horizon at this very present time, but I believe it because I believe the sun will shine tomorrow. I believe it because I believe the rivers are going to run down from the mountains and empty themselves into the ocean to the end of time. I believe it because I believe the mountains are firmly fixed in their foundations, and will stand forever as the everlasting hills.

I believe it because I believe in the glory of God shining in the firmament, and the inevitable fulfilment of his every plan and purpose, and I believe that the making of this into the greatest people on earth and the making of this Government into the very best human government, is in the scope and contemplation of His Divine plan.

Not long ago I heard the famous John L. Stoddard lecture on Norway. The lecture was enriched by stereopticon illustrations. The charming story was emphasized by great pictures that brought everything almost in touch. After the speaker had carried us up through all those arms of the sea that press their way between the narrowly divided mountains, he finally threw a picture on the screen which put all previous ones to shame. The audience held its breath, and finally the lecturer said, "and now, my friends, here we stand at the great North Cape itself." The picture was grand. Behind that giant rock was the threshold of a continent, and before it was the vast Arctic Sea blushing beneath the warm glow of the midnight sun, which never sets, but pauses just above the horizon, as if to let the past embrace the present, and yesterday kiss today. But there came to my mind another picture, which if I had a lantern as faithful to my fancy as Stoddard's was to the wondrous sights he had seen, I would fling for you a picture on this great screen, and show you what I think I see in a not far distant day, when this great nation of God's people shall have been bound together, and been taught to live as brethren dwelling together in unity. I would have them all mustered together, camping out, as it were, in a great union of fellowship, betoking oneness of interest and oneness of destiny, and above them that flag of flags, in which, by a strange coincidence, the story of the nation seems to have been caught in symbol, having, as it does, the red stripes, symbolic color of the blood of earth, and the blue above which is heaven's own color, and running between, the virgin stripes of white, speaking of purity and peace; showing that this people will come together in spirit and truth, and in their unity will march forward from earth to God, singing loud hosannas. "Blessed is the people whose God is the Lord." And then if out of the Milky Way of the white stripes there should shoot forth now and then some new star, it would be to magnify that great constellation in the firmament of nations, which will go on shining forever and forever, differing no more, "save as one star differeth from another star in glory."